NEW AND EXPECTANT MOTHE

A guide for employers

HSE BOOKS

ISBN 0 7176 0826 3

Enquiries regarding this or any other HSE publication should be
made to the HSE Information Centre at the following address:

HSE Information Centre, Broad Lane, Sheffield S3 7HQ
Tel: 0114 2892345, Fax: 0114 2892333

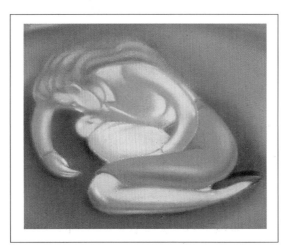

page 1................... **INTRODUCTION**

page 2.................. General duties for all employees

page 3.................. Definitions

page 3.................. **WHAT YOU NEED TO DO**

page 3.................. Look for the hazards

page 4.................. Decide who might be harmed, and how

page 4.................. Tell your employees about the risk

page 4.................. Avoid the risk

page 5.................. Keep the risks under review

page 7.................. **NIGHT WORK**

page 8.................. **HAZARDS, RISKS AND WAYS OF AVOIDING THEM**

(Including physical, chemical and biological agents and

working conditions listed in Annexes 1 and 2 to the

EC Directive on Pregnant Workers (92/85/EEC)

page 36................. **APPENDIX 1** Aspects of pregnancy that may affect work

page 37................. **APPENDIX 2** Removal from risk

page 40................. **APPENDIX 3** References and further reading

C O N T E N T S

This publication is a guide for employers on protecting the health and safety of workers who are new or expectant mothers

INTRODUCTION

1   Pregnancy should not be equated with ill health. It should be regarded as part of everyday life and its health and safety implications can be adequately addressed by normal health and safety management procedures. Many women work while they are pregnant, and many return to work while they are still breastfeeding. Some hazards in the workplace may affect the health and safety of new and expectant mothers and of their children.

General duties for all employers

2   The law at present requires you to assess risks to all your employees, including new and expectant mothers, and to do what is reasonably practicable to control those risks. Exposure limits for hazardous substances and other agents are set at levels which should not put a pregnant or breastfeeding worker, or her child, at risk. In some cases, there are lower exposure levels for pregnant workers, or for women of childbearing capacity, than for other workers.

3   New legislation required to implement the European Directive on Pregnant Workers was introduced into the Management of Health and Safety at Work Regulations 1992 (SI No 2051) by the Management of Health and Safety at Work (Amendment) Regulations 1994 (SI No 2865) with effect from 1 December 1994. It specifically requires you to take particular account of risks to new and expectant mothers when assessing risks in your work activity. If you cannot avoid a risk by other means, you will need to make changes to working conditions or hours, offer suitable alternative work, or if that is not possible give the worker paid leave for as long as necessary to protect her health or safety or that of her child. The legislation that requires you to take this action is set out in Appendix 2. The new Regulations provide that you need to do this when you have been told in writing that a worker is pregnant. They also provide for you to request in writing a certificate from a registered medical practitioner, or a registered midwife, confirming the pregnancy.

4   This guidance sets out the known risks to new and expectant mothers and gives you advice on what you need to do to comply with the law. Appendix 1 sets out some of the features of pregnancy which you may want to take into account in considering your arrangements for pregnant and breastfeeding workers, though you are not required by law to do so.

Definitions

5   The phrase 'new or expectant mother' means a worker who is pregnant, who has given birth within the previous six months, or who is breastfeeding. 'Given birth' is defined in the new Regulations as 'delivered a living child or, after 24 weeks of pregnancy, a stillborn child'.

WHAT YOU NEED TO DO

6   In assessing risks to your employees you need to pay attention to workers who are new or expectant mothers, and to take action to ensure that they are not exposed to any significant risk. Risks include those to the unborn child or child of a woman who is still breastfeeding - not just risks to the mother herself.   You can get advice on carrying out a risk assessment from HSE's free leaflet 5 *Steps to Risk Assessment.*

Look for the hazards

7   Physical, biological and chemical agents, processes and working conditions which may affect the health and safety of new or expectant mothers are set out in the table on pages 8 to 35. They include possible hazards listed in annexes to the European Directive on the health and safety of pregnant workers; the new regulations refer to the annexes.

page 3

8   Many of the hazards included in the table are already covered by specific health and safety regulations, for example Control of Lead at Work Regulations, Control of Substances Hazardous to Health Regulations (COSHH). If any of these hazards are present in your workplace, you should refer to the relevant regulations for information on what you should do - Appendix 3 contains a list of useful guidance.

Decide who might be harmed, and how

9   Your risk assessment may show that there is a substance or work process in your workplace that could damage the health or safety of new or expectant mothers or their children. You need to bear in mind that there could be different risks depending whether workers are pregnant, have recently given birth, or are breastfeeding.

Tell your employees about the risk

10   If your assessment does reveal a risk you should tell female employees of child-bearing capacity about the potential risks if they are, or could in the future be pregnant or breastfeeding. You should also explain what you will do to make sure that new and expectant mothers are not exposed to the risks that could cause them harm. You can also give the information to employee representatives.

Avoid the risk

11   If you have identified a significant risk to the health or safety of a new or expectant mother, you need to decide what action to take. There may be a significant risk, say from a chemical which is covered by the COSHH Regulations. If so, you will normally be doing enough if you follow the requirements of the specific regulations. As a general rule you should in all cases consider removing the hazard or seek to prevent exposure to the risk. Where this is not feasible the risk should be controlled.

12   If there is still a significant risk at work to the safety or health of a new or expectant mother, which goes beyond the level of risk to be expected outside the workplace, then you must take the following steps to remove her from the risk (the legislation that requires you to do this is reproduced in Appendix 2):

Step 1:   temporarily adjust her working conditions and/or hours of work; or if it is not reasonable to do so, or would not avoid the risk

Step 2:   offer her suitable alternative work if any is available; or if that is not feasible, you must

Step 3:   suspend her from work (give her paid leave) for as long as necessary to protect her safety or health or that of her child.

13   These actions are only necessary where as the result of a risk assessment there is genuine concern: if there is any doubt, you may want to seek professional advice on what the risks are and whether they arise from work before offering alternative employment or paid leave.

Keep the risks under review

14   You will need to keep your risk assessments for new or expectant mothers under review. Although any hazards are likely to remain constant, the possibility of damage to the foetus as a result of a hazard will vary at different stages of pregnancy. There are different risks to consider for workers who are breastfeeding.

15   You need to ensure that workers who are breastfeeding are not exposed to risks that could damage health or safety for as long as they continue to breastfeed. The new Regulations do not put a time limit on

breastfeeding. While many women may stop after the first six weeks, the Department of Health recommends exclusive breastfeeding for the first four to six months. After that time, breastfeeding can be continued with advantage, together with the safe introduction of solid food. It is for women themselves to decide for how long they wish to breastfeed, depending on individual circumstances. Although there is no legal requirement to do so, you will want to consider providing a safe and healthy environment for workers who are breastfeeding to express and store milk. The Workplace (Health, Safety and Welfare) Regulations 1992 require suitable facilities to be provided for workers who are pregnant or breastfeeding to rest.

16   Where workers continue to breastfeed for many months after birth, you will want to review the risks regularly. Where you identify risks, you will need to continue to follow the three steps to avoid exposure to the risk, that is adjustment of working hours/conditions, alternative work or paid leave, for as long as it threatens the health and safety of a breastfeeding worker or her child. The main concern is exposure to lead which can enter breast milk. Where employers are controlling risks in line with regulations, it is unlikely that workers who continue breastfeeding will be exposed to risks which give rise to the need for them to be offered alternative work or given paid leave. If you have any doubts, you may wish to call on professional advice from occupational health specialists.

NIGHT WORK

17   You need to give special consideration to new and expectant mothers who work at night. The new Regulations require that if an employee who is a new or expectant mother works at night, and has a medical certificate stating that night work could affect her health or safety, you must either:

Step 1:   offer her suitable alternative daytime work if any is available; or if that is not reasonable

Step 2:   suspend her from work (give her paid leave) for as long as is necessary to protect her health or safety.

18   You are required to take these steps only if the risk arises from work. HSE experts are not at present aware of any risks to pregnant or breastfeeding workers or their children from working at night *per se*. If one of your employees states that she cannot work nights, and if there is a question as to whether the cause arises from her work, you may wish to seek advice from occupational health specialists.

HAZARDS, RISKS, AND WAYS OF AVOIDING THEM
(Including physical, chemical and biological agents and working conditions listed

List of agents/working conditions	What is the risk?
PHYSICAL AGENTS - where these are regarded as agents causing foetal lesions and/or likely to disrupt placen	
Shocks, vibration or movement	Regular exposure to shocks, low frequency vibration, for example driving or riding in off-road vehicles, or excessive movement, may increase the risk of a miscarriage. Long-term exposure to vibration does not cause foetal abnormalities but often occurs with heavy physical work, so there may be an increased risk of prematurity or low birth weight.
Manual handling of loads where there is a risk of injury	Pregnant workers are especially at risk from manual handling injury - for example hormonal changes can affect the ligaments, increasing susceptibility to injury; and postural problems may increase as the pregnancy progresses. There can also be risks for those who have recently given birth, for example after a caesarean section there is likely to be a temporary limitation on lifting and handling capability. There is no evidence to suggest that breastfeeding mothers are at greater risk from manual handling injury than any other workers.

How to avoid the risk	Other legislation
achment, and in particular:	
Pregnant workers and those who have recently given birth are advised to avoid work likely to involve uncomfortable whole body vibration, especially at low frequencies, or where the abdomen is exposed to shocks or jolts. Breastfeeding workers are at no greater risk than other workers.	None specific.
The changes an employer should make will depend on the risks identified in the assessment and the circumstances of the business. For example it may be possible to alter the nature of the task so that risks from manual handling are reduced for all workers including new or expectant mothers. Or it may be necessary to address the specific needs of the worker and reduce the amount of physical work, or provide aids for her in future to reduce the risks she faces.	Manual Handling Operations Regulations 1992 require employers to: ● avoid the need for hazardous manual handling, so far as is reasonably practicable; ● assess the risks from those operations that cannot be avoided; and ● take steps to reduce these risks to the lowest level reasonably practicable.

List of agents/working conditions	What is the risk?
PHYSICAL AGENTS *continued*	
Noise	There appears to be no specific risk to new or expectant mothers or to the foetus, but prolonged exposure to loud noise may lead to increased blood pressure and tiredness. No particular problems for women who have recently given birth or who are breastfeeding.
Ionising Radiation	Significant exposure to ionising radiation can be harmful to the foetus and this is recognised by placing limits on the external radiation dose to the abdomen of the expectant mother for the declared term of her pregnancy. If a nursing mother works with radioactive liquids or dusts, these can cause exposure of the child, particularly through contamination of the mother's skin. Also, there may be a risk to the foetus from significant amounts of radioactive contamination breathed in or ingested by the mother and transferred across the placenta.

Radiation protection policy for all workers, including pregnant women and nursing mothers, is currently being reviewed in the light of

How to avoid the risk	Other legislation
The requirements of the Noise at Work Regulations 1989 should be sufficient to meet the needs of new or expectant mothers.	Noise at Work Regulations 1989 apply to all workers exposed to loud noise where there is a risk to hearing.
Work procedures should be designed to keep exposure of the pregnant woman as low as reasonably practicable and certainly below the statutory dose limit for pregnant women. Special attention should be paid to the possibility of nursing mothers receiving radioactive contamination and they should not be employed in work where the risk of such contamination is high. The working conditions should be such as to make it unlikely that a pregnant woman might receive high accidental exposures to radioactive contamination.	Ionising Radiations Regulations 1985 and supporting Approved Codes of Practice.

revised recommendations from the International Commission on Radiological Protection and dose limits will be changed in due course.

List of agents/working conditions	What is the risk?
PHYSICAL AGENTS *continued*	
Non-ionising electromagnetic radiation (NIEMR)	***Optical radiation:*** Pregnant or breastfeeding mothers are at no greater risk than other workers.
	Electromagnetic fields and waves (eg radio-frequency radiation): Exposure to electric and magnetic fields within current recommendations is not known to cause harm to the foetus or the mother. However, extreme over-exposure to radio-frequency radiation could cause harm by raising body temperature.
Extremes of cold or heat	When pregnant, women tolerate heat less well and may more readily faint or be more liable to heat stress. The risk is likely to be reduced after birth but it is not certain how quickly an improvement comes about. Breastfeeding may be impaired by heat dehydration. No specific problems arise from working in extreme cold, although clearly for other health and safety reasons, warm clothing should be provided.

How to avoid the risk	Other legislation
	None specific.
Exposure to electric and magnetic fields should not exceed the restrictions on human exposure published by the National Radiological Protection Board.	
Pregnant workers should take great care when exposed to prolonged heat at work, for example when working near furnaces. Rest facilities and access to refreshments would help.	None specific.

List of agents/working conditions	What is the risk?
PHYSICAL AGENTS *continued*	
Movements and postures, travelling - either inside or outside the establishment - mental and physical fatigue and other physical burdens connected with the activity of new or expectant mothers	Fatigue from standing and other physical work has long been associated with miscarriage, premature birth and low birth weight. Excessive physical or mental pressure may cause stress and can give rise to anxiety and raised blood pressure. Pregnant workers may experience problems in working at heights, for example ladders, platforms, and in working in tightly fitting workspaces or with workstations which do not adjust sufficiently to take account of increased abdominal size, particularly during the the later stages of pregnancy. This may lead to strain or sprain injuries. Dexterity, agility, co-ordination, speed of movement, reach and balance may also be impaired, and an increased risk of accidents may need to be considered.

How to avoid the risk	Other legislation
Ensure that hours of work and the volume and pacing of work are not excessive and that, where possible, the employees themselves have some control over how their work is organised.

Ensure that seating is available where appropriate.

Longer or more frequent rest breaks will help to avoid or reduce fatigue.

Adjusting workstations or work procedures may help remove postural problems and risk of accidents. | |

List of agents/working conditions	What is the risk?
PHYSICAL AGENTS *continued*	
Work in hyperbaric atmosphere, for example pressurised enclosures and underwater diving	***Compressed air:*** People who work in compressed air are at risk of developing the bends. This is due to free bubbles of gas in the circulation. It is not clear whether pregnant women are more at risk of the bends but potentially the foetus could be seriously harmed by such gas bubbles. For those who have recently given birth there is a small increase in the risk of the bends. There is no physiological reason why a breastfeeding mother should not work in compressed air (although there would be obvious practical difficulties).
	Diving: Pregnant workers are advised not to dive *at all* during pregnancy due to the possible effects of exposure to hyperbaric environment on the foetus. There is no evidence to suggest that breastfeeding and diving are incompatible.

How to avoid the risk	Other legislation
Pregnant workers should not work in compressed air.	Work in Compressed Air Special Regulations 1958 (under revision).
Pregnancy is viewed as a medical reason not to dive. The diving regulations include the provision that if a diver knows of any medical reason why they should not dive, they should disclose it to the dive supervisor and/or refrain from diving. The diving regulations also require all divers to undertake an annual medical examination. In the HSE guidance leaflet on the medical examination of divers, doctors are advised that pregnant workers should not dive.	The Diving Operations at Work Regulations 1981 (to be amended in 1995).

List of agents/working conditions	What is the risk?
BIOLOGICAL AGENTS	
Any biological agent of hazard groups 2,3 and 4 (Categorisation of biological agents according to hazard and categories of containment - Advisory Committee on Dangerous Pathogens)	Many biological agents within the three risk groups can affect the unborn child if the mother is infected during pregnancy. These may be transmitted through the placenta while the child is in the womb, or during or after birth, for example through breastfeeding or through close physical contact between mother and child. Examples of agents where the child might be infected in one of these ways are hepatitis B, HIV (the AIDS virus), herpes, TB, syphilis, chickenpox and typhoid. For most workers, the risk of infection is not higher at work than from living in the community; but in certain occupations, exposure to infections is more likely, for example laboratory workers, health care, people looking after animals and dealing with animal products.
Biological agents known to cause abortion of the foetus, or physical and neurological damage. These agents are included in hazard groups 2, 3 and 4	Rubella (German measles) and toxoplasma can harm the foetus, as can some other biological agents, for example cytomegalovirus (an infection common in the community) and chlamydia in sheep. The risks of infection are generally no higher for workers than others, except in those exposed occupations (see above).

How to avoid the risk	Other legislation
Depends on the risk assessment, which will take account first of the nature of the biological agent, how infection is spread, how likely contact is, and what control measures there are. These may include physical containment, hygiene measures, use of available vaccines if exposure justifies this. If there is a known high risk of exposure to a highly infectious agent, then it will be appropriate for the pregnant worker to avoid exposure altogether.	Control of Substances Hazardous to Health Regulations 1994; Approved Code of Practice on the control of biological agents; approved list of biological agents.
See above.	See above.

List of agents/working conditions	What is the risk?
CHEMICAL AGENTS - The following chemical agents in so far as it is known that they endanger the health	
Substances labelled R40, R45, R46 and R47 under Directive 67/548/EEC [since amended or adapted on a number of occasions]	There are about 200 substances labelled with these risk phrases: R40: possible risk of irreversible effects R45: may cause cancer R46: may cause heritable genetic damage R47: may cause birth defects - this is due to be replaced in 1994/95 by the risk phrases: R61: may cause harm to the unborn child R63: possible risk of harm to the unborn child R64: may cause harm to breastfed babies The actual risk to health of these substances can only be determined following a risk assessment of a particular substance at the place of work - ie although the substances listed may have the potential to endanger health or safety, there may be no risk in practice, for example if exposure is below a level which might cause harm.

How to avoid the risk	Other legislation
egnant women and the unborn child:	
With the exception of lead (see below) and asbestos these substances all fall within the scope of COSHH. For work with hazardous substances, which include chemicals which may cause heritable genetic damage, employers are required to assess the health risks to workers arising from such work, and where appropriate prevent or control the risks. In carrying out assessments employers should have regard for women who are pregnant, or who have recently given birth.	Control of Substances Hazardous to Health Regulations (COSHH). Chemicals (Hazard Information and Packaging) Regulations 1993 (CHIP).

List of agents/working conditions	What is the risk?
CHEMICAL AGENTS *continued*	
Chemical agents and industrial processes in Annex 1 to Directive 90/394/EEC	The substances, preparations and processes listed in Annex 1 also covered by COSHH (see above).
Mercury and mercury derivatives	Organic mercury compounds could have adverse effects on the foetus. Animal studies and human observations have demonstrated that exposure to these forms of mercury during pregnancy can slow the growth of the unborn baby, disrupt the nervous system, and cause the mother to be poisoned. No clear evidence of adverse effects on developing foetus from studies of humans exposed to mercury and inorganic mercury compounds. No indication that mothers are more likely to suffer greater adverse effects from mercury and its compounds after the birth of the baby. Potential for health effects in children from exposure of mother to mercury and mercury compounds is uncertain.

How to avoid the risk	Other legislation
e EC Directive on the Control of Carcinogenic Substances are	COSHH (see above).
Guidance Notes EH17: *Mercury - health and safety precautions* MS12: *Mercury - medical surveillance* give practical guidance on the risks of working with mercury and how to control them.	Mercury and mercury derivatives are covered by the requirements of COSHH.

List of agents/working conditions	What is the risk?
CHEMICAL AGENTS *continued*	
Antimitotic (cytotoxic) drugs	In the long term these drugs cause damage to genetic information in sperm and eggs. Some can cause cancer. Absorption is by inhalation or through the skin.

How to avoid the risk	Other legislation
There is no known threshold limit and exposure must be reduced to as low a level as is reasonably practicable. Assessment of the risk should look particularly at preparation of the drug for use (pharmacists, nurses), administration of the drug, and disposal of waste (chemical and human). Those who are trying to conceive a child or are pregnant or breastfeeding should be fully informed of the reproductive hazard. HSE's Guidance Note MS21 *Precautions for the safe handling of cytotoxic drugs* gives information about the health hazards and advice on avoidance/reduction of risk.	COSHH.

List of agents/working conditions	What is the risk?
CHEMICAL AGENTS *continued*	
Chemical agents of known and dangerous percutaneous absorption (ie that may be absorbed through the skin). This includes some pesticides.	The HSE guidance booklet EH40 *Occupational exposure limits*, updated annually, contains tables of inhalation exposure limits for certain hazardous substances. Some of these substances can also penetrate intact skin and become absorbed into the body, causing ill-health effects. These substances are marked 'Sk' in the tables. As with all substances, the risks will depend on the way that the substance is being used as well as on its hazardous properties. Absorption through the skin can result from localised contamination, for example from a splash on the skin or clothing, or in certain cases, from exposure to high atmospheric concentrations of vapour.

How to avoid the risk	Other legislation
Take special precautions to prevent skin contact. Where possible, use engineering methods to control exposure in preference to personal protective equipment, such as gloves, overalls or face shields. For example perhaps you could enclose the process or redesign it so that less spray is produced. Where you must use personal protective equipment (either alone or in combination with engineering methods), ensure that it is suitable. The Control of Pesticides Regulations 1986 (COPR), sets out general restrictions on the way that pesticides can be used. In addition all pesticides must be approved before they can be advertised, sold, supplied, used or stored. Conditions can be put onto the approval, which may for example limit the way the product can be used (for example restrict the way that it can be applied), require that certain safety precautions are followed, and restrict who may use it (for example professionals or amateurs). These conditions are reflected on the product label. Failure to comply is an offence.	COSHH (see above). Control of Pesticides Regulations 1986 (COPR).

List of agents/working conditions	What is the risk?
CHEMICAL AGENTS *continued*	
Carbon monoxide	Carbon monoxide readily crosses the placenta and can result in the foetus being starved of oxygen. Data on the effects of exposure to carbon monoxide on pregnant women are limited but there is evidence of adverse effects on the foetus. Both the level and duration of maternal exposure are important factors in the effect on the foetus.

There is no indication that breastfed babies suffer adverse effects from their mother's exposure to carbon monoxide, nor that the mother is significantly more sensitive to carbon monoxide after giving birth. |

How to avoid the risk	Other legislation
HSE's guidance note EH43: *Carbon monoxide* - gives practical advice on the risks of working with carbon monoxide and how to control them. It warns that pregnant women may have heightened susceptibility to the effects of exposure to carbon monoxide.	None specific - except for the general requirements of COSHH in relation to hazardous substances.

List of agents/working conditions	What is the risk?
CHEMICAL AGENTS *continued*	
Lead and lead derivatives - in so far as these agents are capable of being absorbed by the human organism	Occupational exposure to lead in the early 1900s, when exposure was poorly controlled, was associated with high frequencies of spontaneous abortion, stillbirth and infertility. More recent studies draw attention to an association between low-level lead exposure before the baby is born from environmental sources and mild decreases in intellectual performance in childhood. The effects on breastfed babies of their mothers' lead exposure have not been studied. However, lead can enter breast milk. Since it is thought that the nervous system of young children is particularly sensitive to the toxic effects of lead, the exposure of breastfeeding mothers to lead should be viewed with concern.

How to avoid the risk	Other legislation
The Approved Code of Practice associated with the lead regulations *Control of lead at work* sets out the current exposure limits for lead and the maximum permissible blood lead levels for workers who are exposed to lead to such a degree that they are subject to medical surveillance. It gives a blood lead level for men and a lower level for women of reproductive capacity. This lower level is set to help ensure that women who may become pregnant have low blood lead levels. This is to help protect the foetus from injury in the weeks before a pregnancy is confirmed. Once their pregnancy is confirmed, women who are subject to medical surveillance under the lead regulations will normally be suspended from work which exposes them significantly to lead, by the Employment Medical Adviser or Appointed Doctor carrying out the medical surveillance.	Control of Lead at Work Regulations 1980 (CLAW) (Currently under review).

List of agents/working conditions	What is the risk?
WORKING CONDITIONS	
Underground mining work	Mines often have difficult physical conditions and many of the physical agents described in this guidance are a regular part of the mining environment.
Work with Display Screen Equipment (VDUs)	Although not specifically listed in the Pregnant Workers Directi on pregnant women has been widespread. However, there Protection Board, which has the statutory function of provid summarises scientific understanding - The levels of ionising and non-ionising electromagnetic radiation which are likely to be generated by display screen equipment are well below those set out in international recommendations for limiting risk to human health created by such emissions and the National Radiological Protection Board does not consider such levels to pose a significant risk to health. No special protective measures are therefore needed to protect the health of people from this radiation.

How to avoid the risk	Other legislation
Managers and contractors are responsible for assessing risks and should take action in line with suggestions elsewhere in this table.	

E is aware that anxiety about radiation emissions from display screen equipment and possible effects
stantial evidence that these concerns are unfounded. The HSE has consulted the National Radiological
ormation and advice on all radiation matters to Government Departments, and the advice below

How to avoid the risk	Other legislation
In the light of the scientific evidence pregnant women do not need to stop work with VDUs. However, to avoid problems caused by stress and anxiety, women who are pregnant or planning children and worried about working with VDUs should be given the opportunity to discuss their concerns with someone adequately informed of current authoritative scientific information and advice.	Display Screen Equipment Regulations 1992.

List of agents/working conditions	What is the risk?
WORKING CONDITIONS *continued*	
Work with Display Screen Equipment (VDUs) *continued*	There has been considerable public concern about reports of higher levels of miscarriage and birth defects among some groups of visual display unit (VDU) workers, in particular due to electromagnetic radiation. Many scientific studies have been carried out, but taken as a whole their results do not show any link between miscarriages or birth defects and working with VDUs. Research and reviews of the scientific evidence will continue to be undertaken.

How to avoid the risk	Other legislation

APPENDIX 1 - Aspects of pregnancy that may affect work

Apart from the hazards listed in the table, there are other aspects of pregnancy that may affect work. The impact will vary during the course of the pregnancy and you will want to keep their effects under review, for example the posture of expectant mothers changes to cope with increasing size.

Aspects of pregnancy	*Factors in work*
Morning sickness	Early shift work
	Exposure to nauseating smells
Backache	Standing/manual handling/posture
Varicose veins	Standing/sitting
Haemorrhoids	Working in hot conditions
Frequent visits to toilet	Difficulty in leaving job/site of work
Increasing size	Use of protective clothing
	Work in confined areas
	Manual handling
Tiredness	Overtime
	Evening work
Balance	Problems of working on slippery, wet surfaces
Comfort	Problems of working in tightly fitting workspaces
Dexterity, agility, co-ordination, speed of movement, reach, may be impaired because of increasing size.	

APPENDIX 2 - Removal from risk

The guidance has explained the steps you should take when it is necessary to remove a new or expectant mother from a significant risk. The legislation that requires you to take action is as follows. (References to the Management of Health and Safety at Work Regulations are to those Regulations as amended - see paragraph 3 of this guidance.)

Step 1

Management of Health and Safety at Work Regulations Regulation 13A(2): requires, as the first possibility, the employee's working conditions and/or hours of work to be temporarily adjusted.

Step 2

Employment Protection (Consolidation) Act 1978 Section 46: if Step 1 is not reasonable or would not avoid the risk, a new or expectant mother has a right to be offered suitable alternative work, if any is available.

The work must be:

- both suitable and appropriate for her to do in the circumstances; and

- on terms and conditions no less favourable than her normal terms and conditions.

An employee is entitled to make a complaint to an Industrial Tribunal if there is suitable alternative work available which her employer has failed to offer to her before suspending her from work on maternity grounds.

Step 3

Management of Health and Safety at Work Regulations Regulation 13A(3): if suitable alternative work cannot be provided, then the employee must be suspended from work.

Employment Protection (Consolidation) Act 1978 Sections 45 and 47: an employee suspended from work on these grounds is entitled to be paid remuneration - that is, wages or salary - at her full normal rate for as long as the suspension continues. The only exception is where she has unreasonably refused an offer of suitable alternative work, in which case no remuneration is payable for the period during which the offer applies.

If an employee has both a statutory right and a contractual right to remuneration during maternity suspension, such entitlements can be offset against each other.

The employee continues to be employed during the maternity suspension period, which therefore counts towards her period of continuous employment for the purposes of assessing seniority, pension rights and other personal length-of-service payments, such as pay increments. There is however no statutory requirement for contractual benefits apart from remuneration to be continued during the maternity suspension itself. This, like most other terms and conditions of employment, remains a matter for negotiation and agreement on a voluntary or contractual basis between the parties concerned. Employers should however ensure that they are not acting unlawfully under the Equal Pay Act 1970 and the Sex Discrimination Act 1975.

An employee whose employer fails to pay her some or all of the remuneration due for any day of maternity suspension is entitled to make a complaint to an Industrial Tribunal.

Night work

Step 1

Employment Protection (Consolidation) Act 1978 Sections 45 and 47: if an employee has a medical certificate stating that night work could affect her health or safety, she has a right to be offered suitable alternative daytime work on terms and conditions no less favourable than her normal terms and conditions.

Step 2

Management of Health and Safety at Work Regulations Regulation 13B: if it is not possible to offer the employee suitable alternative daytime work, then she must be suspended from work.

Employment Protection (Consolidation) Act 1978 Sections 45 and 47: provide for suspension from work to be on full pay (see Step 3 above).

You can obtain further information from *Maternity Rights - à guide for employers and employees* Employment Department Group PL958, available free of charge from offices of the Employment Service.

Appendix 3 - References and further reading

Carbon monoxide HSE Guidance Note EH43 1984 ISBN 0 11 883597 1

Control of lead at work Approved Code of Practice (rev) 1985 ISBN 0 11 883780 X

COSHH: a brief guide for employers IND(G)136(L) 1993 Free leaflet

5 steps to risk assessment Free leaflet IND(G)163(L)

Getting to grips with manual handling. A short guide for employers Free leaflet IND(G)143(L)

Introducing the Noise at Work Regulations - a brief guide to the requirements for controlling noise at work
IND(G)75(L) Free leaflet

Management of Health and Safety at Work Approved Code of Practice L21
1992 ISBN 0 7176 0412 8

Manual Handling Operations Regulations 1992. Guidance on Regulations L23
1992 ISBN 0 7176 0411 X

Mercury - health and safety precautions HSE Guidance Note EH17 1977 ISBN 0 11 883176 3

Mercury - medical surveillance HSE Guidance Note MS12 1978 ISBN 0 11 883191 7

Occupational exposure limits HSE Guidance Note EH40/94 1994 ISBN 0 7176 0722 4

Personal Protective Equipment at Work Regulations 1992. Guidance on Regulations L25
1992 ISBN 0 7176 0415 2

Precautions for the safe handling of cytotoxic drugs HSE Guidance Note MS21
1983 ISBN 0 11 883571 8

VDUs: An easy guide to the Regulations HS(G)90 1994 ISBN 0 7176 0735 6

Printed and published by the Health and Safety Executive   12/94   C100